Political

BOLLOCKS

Aubrey Malone

Published in the UK by
POWERFRESH Limited
Unit 3, Everdon Park,
Heartlands Industrial Estate,
Daventry
NN11 5YJ

Telephone   01327 871 777
Facsimile   01327 879 222
E Mail info@powerfresh.co.uk

ISBN   1904967027

Printed in Malta by Gutenberg Press Ltd
Powerfresh September 2004

Aubrey Malone, was born in Co Mayo in 1953. He moved to Dublin in 1969, attending Belvedere College and then UCD where he studied English and Philosophy before going on to become a teacher. He published a short story collection, Flight, in 1980. Since then he has worked mainly in journalism, having been a feature writer and reviewer of movies and books for most of the national newspapers and magazines at one time or another on a freelance basis. Married, he lives in Dublin.

Amongst Aubrey's numerous publications are: Hollyweird (Michael O'Mara books), a compilation of Hollywood-related trivia; The Brothers Behan (Blackhall), a biography of Brian and Brendan Behan; the best-selling The Cynic's Dictionary (Prion); Historic Pubs of Dublin (New Island); and a biography of Ernest Hemingway, Hemingway: The Grace and the Pressure (Robson Books), Little Books The Big 40, 50, 60 as well as Turning 18 (Powerfresh).

To all the Politicians who did to their countries what John F. Kennedy did to Marilyn Monroe.

POLITICIANS' LIES
(Real Meaning in Brackets)

"What do you mean I said the opposite last week?". *(Give me a minute to get an excuse ready)*

"I'll let my colleague answer that". *(...because I'm stumped)*

"We're all very excited about this project at the moment". *(Yes folks it's nest-feathering time again)*

"In a few weeks I'll have a better notion of how things are going to pan out". *(I've just landed on a mega-bummer).*

"No, I did not at any time express that intention". *(I didn't think anyone heard me)*

"I'm not at liberty to answer that". *(You've got me with my pants down)*

"I came into this job with a dream". *(...of getting filthy rich)*

"Myself and X have absolutely nothing against one another". *(Each night of our lives we fantasise about seeing each other murdered)*

"It's in the pipeline". *(We scuppered that one, mate)*

"I'll stand by everything I said".(*...until I'm found out*)

"A reliable source informs me". *(That's right, I had another natter with yer man in the pub last night)*

"Ask not what your country can do for you, but what you can do for your country". *(Screw the beleaguered middle income bracket - I'm off to the Canaries)*

"Prove it". *(My ass is covered)*

"Posterity will see me differently". *(My biog. will probably be banned)*

"I'm afraid I can't quote you chapter and verse on that one without my papers". *(This is a total, unmitigated, 18 carat lie I've just told you)*

"I have a sixth sense about this". *(..but I appear to be missing the other five)*

"On mature recollection". *(Guess how many pints I had in the pub last night?)*

"Now you're being silly; that's a preposterous allegation". *(You rotter - where did you dig that info up ?)*

"That would not be an expedient option, I'm afraid". *(I'm too damned lazy to entertain it)*

"My diary is full for the forseeable future". *(I've been having the time of Reilly those past few weeks in Stringfellows)*

"We're on a negative growth curve". *(We're screwed)*

"Would I lie to you?".*(Does the bear poop in the woods ? Is the Pope a Catholic?).*

POLITICAL QUOTES

Every man should have a wife because there are some things you can't blame on the government. *(Hal Roach)*

In a democracy you can say what you like as long as you do what you're told. *(Anthony Butler)*

The cheapest way to have your family tree traced is to go into politics. *(Bob Hope)*

Democracy is too good to share with just anybody. *(H.L. Mencken)*

A politician is a person who has nothing to say but says it anyway. *(Sean Hughes)*

It is now known that men enter local politics solely as a result of being unhappily married. *(C. Northcote Parkinson)*

The wrong sort of people are always in power because they would not be in power if they were not the wrong sort of people. *(Jon Wynne-Tyson)*

All terrorists, at the invitation of the Government, end up with drinks at the Dorchester. *(Hugh Gaskill)*

Ronald Reagan did for monetarism what the Boston Strangler did for door-to-door salesmen. *(Denis Healey)*

Mrs Thatcher tells us she has given the French President a piece of her mind - not a gift I would receive with alacrity. *(Denis Healey)*

When a politician says yes he means maybe. When he says maybe he means no, and when he says no he's no politician. When a lady says no she means maybe. When she says maybe she means yes, but when she says yes she's no lady. *(Edwina Currie)*

Tony Benn has had more roads to Damascus than a Syrian lorry driver. *(Jimmy Reid)*

When Edwina Currie goes to the dentist, he's the one who needs the anaesthetic. *(Frank Dobson)*

Putting Norman Tebbit in charge of industrial relations is like appointing Dracula to take charge of the blood transfusion service. *(Eric Varley)*

I don't often attack the Labour Party - they do it so well themselves. *(Ted Heath)*

If God had been a Liberal, there wouldn't have been Ten Commandments — just ten suggestions. *(Malcolm Bradbury)*

The social Democrats are the world's most boring party. They were born yawning. *(Jon Akass)*

The Tory Party is split into two factions over Nigel Lawson: those who hate him, and those who loathe him. *(Ron Edmonds)*

Tony Benn did more harm to British industry than the combined efforts of the Luftwaffe and the U-boats did in the whole of the last war. *(Cyril Smith)*

Michael Foot looks like a squawking cockatoo, his spiky white strands quivering with indignation as if somebody had just pinched a cuttlefish from his cage.*(James Murray)*

Nero fiddled, but Coolidge only snored. *(H.L. Mencken on Calvin Coolidge)*

Receiving support from Ted Heath in a by-election is like being measured by an undertaker. *(George Gardiner)*

Arthur Scargill couldn't negotiate his way out of a toilet. *(Ray Lynk)*

Margaret Thatcher hijacked the Tory Party from the landowners and gave it to the estate agents. *(Denis Healey)*

No one can be against Michael Heseltine and be all bad. *(Edward Pearce)*

I saw a headline which read 'Denis Healey caught with his pants down' and thought: that will make it easier to hear what he's saying. *(Bob Monkhouse)*

I don't like to attack Ronnie Reagan as being too old to hold office, but let's remember that in his first movie Gabby Hayes got the girl. *(Walter Mondale)*

Pathetic, sectarian, mono-ethnic and mono-cultural. *(David Trimble on the Republic of Ireland in 2002)*

He must have stopped taking the tablets. *(DUP Deputy Leader Peter Robinson on Trimble's outburst).*

John F Kennedy's victory in Wisconsin proves that a millionaire has just as good a chance in politics as anyone else. *(Bob Hope)*

He has the gift of compressing the largest amount of words into the smallest amount of thought. *(Winston Churchill on Ramsey MacDonald)*

He knows nothing but thinks he knows everything. That points clearly to a political career. *(George Bernard Shaw)*

Peter Mandelson is someone who can skulk in broad daylight. *(Simon Hoggart)*

The nice thing about being a celebrity is that when you bore people, they think it's their fault. *(Henry Kissinger)*

When you're skinning your customers, you should leave some skin on to grow so you can skin them again. *(Nikita Khruschev)*

Richard Nixon told us he was going to take crime out of the streets. He did. He took it into the damn White House. *(Ralph Abernathy)*

There's nothing in socialism that a little money won't cure,*(Will Durant)*

The Tory party is the cream of England: rich, thick and full of clots. *(Graffiti)*

Anybody who wants the presidency so much that he'll spend two years canvassing for it is not to be trusted with the office. *(David Broder)*

The first requirement of a statesman is that he be dull. *(Dean Acheson)*

There are three times in a man's life when it's useless to hold him to anything: when he's madly in love, drunk or running for office. *(Robert Mitchum)*

Ask not what your country can do for you. Most of the politicians are corrupt anyway. *(Rita Coolidge)*

Being powerful is like being a lady. If you have to tell people you are, you aren't. *(Jesse Carr)*

Democracy is the worst form of government, except for all the others. *(Winston Churchill)*

I have never derived any pleasure from spanking black girls. It conflicts with my belief in civil liberties. *(Kenneth Tynan)*

The three most useless things in life are a Pope's penis, a nuns vagina and an election promise. *(Anon)*

The vote means nothing to women. We should be armed. *(Edna O'Brien)*

If a man hasn't discovered something that he will die for, he isn't fit to live. *(Martin Luther King)*

There's one good thing about being president - nobody can tell you when you sit down. *(Dwight Eisenhower)*

I never vote for anybody. I always vote against. *(W.C. Fields)*

I never dared to be radical when young for fear it would make me conservative when old. *(Robert Frost)*

Communism is like Prohibition. It's a good idea but it won't work. *(Will Rogers)*

A government which robs Peter to pay Paul can always depend on the support of Paul. *(George Bernard Shaw)*

The cure for admiring The house of Lords is to go and look at it.*(Walter Bagehot)*

The Welfare State should really be called the Farewell State.*(J.B. Priestley)*

Politics is too serious to be left to the politicians. *(Charles de Gaulle)*

Is there life before death? *(Seamus Heaney on the Troubles in Northern Ireland)*

It's not a good idea for a woman to enter politics, it takes too long to do two faces. *(Lily Tomlin)*

A conservative is someone who demands a square deal for the rich. *(David Frost)*

The ideal way of opening Parliament would be to put a bomb under it and press the button. *(P.G. Wodehouse)*

It's not the voting that's democracy; it's the counting. *(Tom Stoppard)*

I'm a Communist by day and a Catholic as soon as it gets dark. *(Brendan Behan)*

Politics is the second oldest profession on earth - and it bears a gross resemblance to the first. *(Ronald Reagan)*

Devolution is the solution to pollution. *(Peer Cagney)*

Liberals understand everything except people who don't understand *them. (Lenny Bruce)*

If I had to choose between betraying my country and betraying my friend, I hope I should have the guts to betray my country. *(E.M. Forster)*

There are two kinds of women: those who want power in the world and those who want power in bed. *(Jacqueline Onassis)*

If you go into a campus these days, people are too busy reading *'The Wall Street Journal' to protest. (Fionnuala Flanagan)*

Free Northern Ireland. Just send six box tops and a self-addressed envelope. *(Graffiti)*

The more you read about politics, you realise that one party is worse than the other. *(Will Rogers)*

When you're abroad you're a statesman. When you're at home you're just a politician. *(Harold Macmillan)*

Politicians, like the Chinese, all look alike. *(Veronica Lake)*

Politicians promise to build a bridge even where there's no river. *(Nikita Khruschev)*

There can be no whitewash at the White House. *(Richard Nixon)*

As with the Christian religion, the worst advertisements for socialism is its adherents. *(George Orwell)*

Every successful revolution puts on in time the robes of the tyrant it has deposed. *(Barbara Tuchman)*

It's a pity that more politicians aren't bastards by birth rather than reputation. *(Katharine Whitehorn)*

Practical politics consists in ignoring facts. *(Henry Brooks Adams)*

History is bunk. *(Henry Ford)*

Don't vote. The government always gets in. *(Adrian Edmondson)*

When you're on the periphery, it's not the periphery it's the centre. *(Mary Robinson)*

Tyranny is always better organised than freedom. *(Charles Peguy)*

Conservatives believe in reform, but not yet. *(Anon)*

'Some Californian people with a lot of money came to me and said they'd support me if I ran for politics. I said if I could play six weeks in Vegas and do two pictures a year, I'd do it.' *(Shirley MacLaine)*

'A country that can put men on the moon can put women in the constitution.' *(Margaret Heckler)*

'Any woman who understands the problems of running a house will be nearer to understanding the problems of running a country.' *(Margaret Thatcher)*

'What's the point of having a vote if there's no one worth voting for?' *(Shirley MacLaine)*

'One does wish that there were a few more women in parliament. Then one could be less conspicuous oneself.' *(Margaret Thatcher)*

'Inside, I am twelve years old. That's why I've never voted. I'm under-age.' *(Sophia Loren, on her 60th birthday in 1994)*

'Philip Guadella once said to me that voting papers should be made so complicated that only the most highly educated liberals could understand them.' *(Mrs Jean V.Saunders)*

'If Labour is the answer, it must have been a bloody silly question.' *(Graffito)*

'We could get quite a lot of governing done, if it wasn't for politics.' *(Helen Simpson)*

If you want to push something in politics, you're accused of being aggressive, and that's not supposed to be a good thing for a woman. If you get upset and show it, you're accused of being emotional. *(Mary Harney)*

My husband said that if I became a politician, it would be grounds for annulment. *(Liz O'Donnell)*

Being an M.P. is the sort of job all working class parents want for their children: clean, indoor and no heavy lifting. *(Diane Abbott, M.P.)*

There's one sure way of telling when politicians aren't telling the truth: their lips move. *(Felicity Kendall)*

Politics will always be run to suit the male agenda. No matter how many strides are made in terms of equality, at the end of the day women are still primarily responsible for the children, for their education, getting the meals on the table, making sure the school uniform is ready for Monday morning. *(Avril Doyle)*

The thing about a politician is, you have to take the smooth with the smooth. *(Susan Hill)*

98% of the adults in America are decent, hard-working and honest. It's the other 2% that get all the publicity. But then - we elected them'. *(Lily Tomlin)*

Nancy Reagan's skin is so tight, every time she crosses her legs, her mouth snaps open. *(Joan Rivers)*

Communists all seem to wear small caps, a look I consider better suited to tubes of toothpaste than people. *(Fran Lebowitz)*

I don't know a lot about politics, but I can recognise a good party man when I see one. *(Mae West)*

If anyone accuses me of being a communist, I'll hit them with my diamond bracelet. *(Pauline Goddard)*

It is well known that the most radical revolutionary will become a conservative on the day after the revolution. *(Hannah Arendt)*

In politics women type the letters, lick the stamps, distribute the pamphlets and get out the vote. Men get elected. *(Claire Boothe Luce)*

There are lies, damned lies, and Roy Hattersley. *(John Vincent)*

A diplomat's life is made up of two ingredients: alcohol and protocol.

(Adlai Stevenson)

POLITICAL JOKES

Government Health Warning:
This government will seriously damage your health.

The only good Tory is a lavatory.

How would you get a hundred senators into a Mini? *Make one of them president and the other 99 will crawl up his arse.*

Why does Bill Clinton rarely listen to his conscience? *He hates taking advice from strangers.*

Ronald Reagan was a Nancy boy.

Richard Nixon was the type of man to cut down an oak tree and then mount the stump and give a lecture on conservation.

When Nancy Reagan was informed her husband had Alzheimer's Disease, she said, 'How can they tell?'

Paddy wasn't very politically aware. When he heard there was to be a Nelson Mandela benefit gig, he went: 'Really, is his stuff any good?'

Get Saddam Hussein before Saddam Hussein gets..............AAAAAAAAA AAAAGGGGHHHH

When Bill Clinton was asked what he thought of the Northern Ireland position, he said, 'I don't think I've tried that one. Who goes on top?'

How many Irish Republicans does it take to screw in a lightbulb? *None. Lightbulbs have the right to govern their own future.*

How would you make Ian Paisley dumb? *Delete the word 'no' from the English vocabulary.*

Was Monica Lewinsky to Bill Clinton what Marilyn Monroe was to John F. Kennedy? *Close, but no cigar.*

Hillary Clinton may have been Bill's First Lady, but she won't be his last.

Saddam Hussein has only one bad habit. *He breathes.*

Why does Bill Clinton have a pet name for his penis? *He wants to be on first name terms with the person who makes 99% of his decisions.*

What did George Bush say when his wife blew into his ear? *'Thanks for the re-fill, honey.'*

Why does George Bush never suffer from haemorrhoids? *He's a perfect asshole.*

Maggie Thatcher may have only been a grocer's daughter, but she taught Sir Geoffrey Howe.

Capitalism is survival of the fattest.

Why does Bill Clinton like sex with the light on? *So he can remember who he's screwing.*

Dan Quayle hasn't many faults, but he's sure made the most of the ones he has.

What were the four critical periods in Bill Clinton's administration? *Spring, summer, autumn and winter.*

Gerald Ford couldn't fart and chew gum at the same time.

What's the main similarity between Richard Nixon and Bill Clinton? *They were both destroyed by Deep Throat.*

What does Bill Clinton use for protection when he's having sex? *The Secret Service.*

Chelsey Clinton doesn't know what to make of her parents. Her father can't keep his pants on and her mother wants to wear them.

When Hillary asked Chelsey if she ever had sex, she replied 'Not according to Dad'.

An honest politician is one who, when he's bought, stays bought.

What's Bill Clinton's favourite nursery rhyme? *Hump Me, Dump Me.*

Dan Quayle got an idea the other day but it died of loneliness.

When Chelsey Clinton asked her father if all fairytales began with the words 'Once upon a time" he told her no, that some of them begin with 'I never had sexual relations with that woman'.

Why did Quayle buy a German get-well card for his friend? *Because she had German measles.*

Ulster dyslexics say 'On'.

What is the difference between love and George Bush? *Love is a Cupid stunt.*

What does George Bush feel about Red China? *They generally think it's okay - as long as it doesn't clash with the table-cloth.*

What are Bush's views on the Renault 5? *He thinks they should be released.*

What are Bush's views on Marxism? *He prefers Groucho to Harpo.*

Richard Nixon had such a high regard for the truth, he only used it on special occasions.

Bill Clinton finally got his bill from Monica Lewinsky: Four million dollars for damages and $2.85 for dry cleaning.

A schoolteacher in Ireland was once trying to explain to his class what the difference between a misfortune and a calamity was, and finally hit upon a perfect example.
'If an Orangeman fell into the river Lee' he said, 'that would be a misfortune — but if anyone pulled him out again, that would be a calamity!'

You can make 'The Death' from Ted Heath's name. and 'Grow a Penis from Spiro Agnew's. Are they trying to tell us something?

What's the definition of silence?
*Bill Clinton and Dan Quayle
telling one another Vietnam sto-
ries.*

Dan Quayle brightens up a room
just by leaving it,

Why was John Major like a toilet cleaner? *He got rid of jobs.*

What are the two worst things
about the average politician? *His
faces.*

Denis Thatcher will never be the
man Margaret was.

The ideology of politics in a nutshell:

Conservatism: You have two cows.

Socialism: You have two cows. The government takes them and gives you the milk.

Communism: The government takes your cows and SELLS you the milk.

Capitalism: You sell your cows and buy a bull.

National Socialism: The government takes your cows and shoots you.

Dan Quayle suffered from foot-in-mouth disease, so his spin-doctor told him to think before he spoke. The next time he had a Press Conference he only said one sentence: 'No comment - and don't quote me on that.'

Margaret Thatcher was the best man that was ever in the Tory Party.

Newsflash: John Major was shot dead this afternoon. Doctors say his condition is satisfactory.

Why blame John Major for England's problems? He did nothing!

Is Michael Foot a leg-end in his own lifetime?

If Ian Duncan Smith and Tony Blair fell off a building together, who would reach the ground first? *Who cares?*

What's the difference between a porcupine and the House of Commons? *A porcupine has all the pricks on the outside.*

In what month do the Tory Party have the least amount sex scandals? *February.*

MORE POLITICAL
QUOTES

A sheep in sheep's clothing. *(Winston Churchill on Clement Attlee)*

The Eichmann trial taught the world the banality of evil; Nixon taught it the evil of banality. *(Ivan Stone)*

Not only is he a bore: he bores for England. *(Malcolm Muggeridge on Anthony Eden)*

A pig-eyed bag of wind. *(Frank Howley on Khruschev)*

Richard Nixon can lie out of both sides of his mouth at the same time. If he ever caught himself telling the truth he'd lie just to keep his hand in. *(Harry Truman)*

He occasionally stumbled over the truth, but hastily picked himself up and hurried on as if nothing had happened. *(Winston Churchill on Stanley Baldwin)*

Winston Churchill would make a drum out of the skin of his mother in order to sound his own praises. *(David Lloyd George)*

You look like an Easter Island statue with an arse full of razor blades. *(Paul Keating to Malcolm Fraser)*

Better to have him inside the tent pissing out than outside pissing in. *(Lyndon Johnson on the necessity of being friendly with J. Edgar Hoover)*

The vice-presidency of America isn't worth a pitcher of warm piss. *(John Gardner to Lyndon Johnson)*

I don't make jokes. I just watch the government and report the facts. *(Will Rogers)*

Do you realise the responsibility I carry? I'm the only man standing between Nixon and the White House. *(John F. Kennedy)*

He played too much football without a helmet. *(Lyndon Johnson on Gerald Ford)*

The Catholics have been interfering in Ulster affairs since 1641. *(Ian Paisley)*

Harold Wilson is going around the country stirring up apathy. *(William Whitelaw)*

Oh if I could piss the way he speaks. *(Georges Clemenceau on David Lloyd George)*

Everytime Richard Nixon left the White House they checked the silverware. *(Woody Allen)*

An empty suit that goes to funerals and plays golf. *(Ross Perot on Dan Quayle)*

Al Gore is in danger of becoming all things to no people. *(Paul Bograd)*

Reader: Suppose you were an idiot. And suppose you were a Member of Congress. But I repeat myself. *(Mark Twain)*

In America any boy may become president. It's just one of the risks he takes. *(Adlai Stevenson)*

An improbable creature, like a human giraffe sniffing down his nostrils at mortals beneath his gaze. *(Richard Wilson on De Gaulle)*

In a disastrous fire in Ronald Reagan's library, both books were destroyed. Sadly, one of them wasn't even coloured in. *(Jonathan Hunt)*

A sophistical rhetorician, inebriated with the exuberance of his own verbosity. *(Benjamin Disraeli on Gladstone)*

One could not even dignify him with the name of stuffed shirt. He was simply a hole in the air. *(George Orwell on Stanley Baldwin)*

Why should white Rhodesians give up everything for some half-baked untried theory of one man, one vote? *(Conservative MP John Stokes in 1965)*

They're all the same. They're short, they're fat, they're slimy and they're fundamentally corrupt. *(Conservative minister Rod Richards on Welsh labour councillors in 1994)*

When the president does it, that means it's not illegal. *(Richard Nixon's 'excuse' for Watergate as spoken to David Frost in an interview in 1977)*

If the Republicans stop telling lies about the Democrats, we'll stop telling the truth about them. *(Adlai Stevenson)*

The worst thing you can call Paul Keating is, frankly, Paul Keating. *(John Hewson)*

Any practical statesman will, under duress, swallow a dozen oaths to get his hand on the driving wheel. *(George Bernard Shaw)*

He's the only major politician in this country who can be labelled 'liar' without fear of libel. *(Joseph Alsop on Joe McCarthy)*

He looked at me as if I were a side dish he hadn't ordered. *(Ring Lardner on President W.H. Taft)*

I've noticed that everybody who is in favour of abortion has already been born. *(Ronald Reagan)*

His impact on history is nothing more than the whiff of scent on a lady's handkerchief. *(David Lloyd George on Arthur Balfour)*

He hasn't a single redeeming defect. *(Benjamin Disraeli on William Gladstone)*

We are not at war with Egypt. We are in a state of armed conflict. *(British PM Anthony Eden on the invasion of the Suez Canal in 1956).*

The only way to combat criminals is by refusing to vote for them. *(Dayton Allen)*

It was so cold I saw a politician with his hands in his own pockets. *(Henny Youngman)*

I didn't just screw Ho Chi Minh; I cut his pecker off. *(Lyndon B. Johnson being rather presumptuous about the Vietnam war in 1964 after bombing Hanoi)*

He looked at foreign affairs through the wrong end of a municipal drainpipe. *(Winston Churchill on Neville Chamberlain)*

A government which robs Peter to pay Paul can always depend on the support of Paul. *(George Bernard Shaw)*

The nine most terrifying words in the English language are, 'I'm from the government and I'm here to help.' *(Ronald Reagan)*

Franco's funeral! *(Brendan Behan after being asked what he would most like to see when he went to Spain)*

I thought he was a young man of promise, but it appears he was a young man of promises. *(Arthur Balfour on Churchill)*

The world would not be in such a snarl, Had Marx been born Groucho instead of Karl. *(Irving Berlin)*

That slick, draft-dodging, dope-smoking, no inhaling, philandering, Elvis-worshipping, Moscow-visiting, special-interest-catering, Big Mac loving, hen-pecked, fork-tongued Ivy League lawyer. *(Michael Dalton Johnson on Bill Clinton)*

As with the Christian religion, the worst advertisement for socialism is its adherents. *(George Orwell)*

A semi-house-trained polecat. *(Michael Foot on Norman Tebbit)*

Politics are just like women. Get into them seriously and you're going to come out looking like an earthworm stepped on by a longshoreman's boot. *(Charles Bukowski)*

Irish politicians do things every day that politicians in other countries have to resign for. *(Dermot Bolger)*

Politicians suffer from intellectual constipation and emotional diarrhoea. *(Michael Considine)*

I admire Margaret Thatcher because she has so much balls, but on the other hand she's a tyrannical bloody bitch. *(Charlie McCreevy)*

The only man who really knew how to deal with terrorists in this country was De Valera. He put them up against a wall and shot them. *(Irish politician Brendan McGahon)*

I wish that somebody would give Ian Paisley a present of the map of Ireland. Then he might discover to his astonishment that there are nine counties in Ulster instead of six. *(Con Houlihan)*

An Irish politician's smile is like moonlight on a tombstone. *(Sean Kilroy)*

Ian Paisley has never had a good word to say about anyone other than himself and Jesus Christ, whom he refers to as his Maker - a rather poor testimonial.
(James Cameron)

The best government is a benevolent tyranny tempered by an occasional assassination.
(Voltaire)

The House UnAmerican Activities Committee nail anyone who ever scratched his ass during the National Anthem.
(Humphrey Bogart)

A despot easily forgives his subjects for not loving him, provided they do not love each other.
(Alexis de Tocqueville)

Once in the sixties, Douglas Gageby asked me what I thought of the idea of Haughey as Taoiseach and I said. 'On the condition that I could police his government 24 hours out of 24, to protect him from his friends.'
(John Healy on Charles Haughey the former Irish Tauiseech)

MORE POLITICAL JOKES

Did you hear about the disadvantaged Kennedy? *He grew up with black & white TV.*

How do the Kennedys propose to their girlfriends? *With the line: 'How would you like to be buried with my people?'*

Why would JFK not have made a good boxer? *He couldn't take a shot to the head.*

George Bush thinks El Salvador is a Mexican bullfighter.

"Apart from that, Mrs Kennedy, how did you enjoy the trip to Dallas?"

What's the difference between the Kennedy family and a photocopier? *One makes facsimiles and the other sick families.*

When he was asked about the murder of Nicole Simpson, he announced: 'Personally, I think Bart did it'.

What was Ted Kennedy's advice to Clarence Thomas when Anita Hill accused him of sexual harassment? *'Why not drown the bitch?'*

What did Ted Kennedy say to Mary Jo Kopechne when she told him she was pregnant with his child and was considering having an abortion? *'We'll cross that bridge when we come to it!'*

John F Kennedy, George Bush and Bill Clinton are all aboard the Titanic when it starts to sink. 'Women and children first!' says Bush. 'Fuck the women' says Kennedy. To which Clinton replies: 'Have we time?'

EVEN MORE POLITICAL QUOTES

If John Major was drowning, his whole life would pass before him and he wouldn't be in it. *(Dave Allen)*

I cannot bring myself to vote for a woman who has been voice-trained to speak to me as though my dog has just died. *(Keith Waterhouse on Margaret Thatcher)*

Margaret Thatcher sounded like the Book of Revelation read out over a railways public address system by a headmistress of a certain age wearing calico knickers. *(Clive James)*

In any civilised country, Ted Heath would have been left hanging upside down on a petrol pump years ago. *(Auberon Waugh)*

People think I sit here and push buttons all day to get things done. That's not how it works. I spent all day today, for instance, kissing behinds. *(Harry S. Truman)*

The White House has had no involvement in this particular incident. *(Richard Nixon shortly after news of the Watergate break-in was linked to him).*

Power corrupts, but lack of power corrupts absolutely. *(Adlai Stevenson)*

I don't give a shit what happens. I want you all to stonewall it. Let them plead the Fifth Amendment, cover up, anything else if it'll save the plan. *(Nixon a few months later)*

Michael Heseltine couldn't see a parapet without ducking beneath it. *(Julian Critchley)*

We built our gas chambers to accommodate 2000 people at a time. *(Rudolph Hess)*

Every reformation must have its victims. You can't expect the fatted calf to share the enthusiasm of the angels over the prodigal's return. *(Saki)*

The only man who had a proper understanding of parliament was Guy Fawkes. *(George Bernard Shaw)*

Politics is the chloroform of the Irish people - or rather the hashish. *(Oliver St John Gogarty)*

He could bury his grandmother in concrete and you would still sympathise with him. *(Neil Jordan on Michael Collins)*

There's only one way to leave power, and that's kicking and screaming. *(P.J. Mara)*

The function of socialism is to raise suffering to a higher level. *(Norman Mailer)*

Politicians are like nappies. They should be changed often - and for the same reason. *(Patrick Murray)*

I have met garbage men with more soul than President Johnson. *(Charles Bukowski)*

Socialism is nothing but the capitalism of the lower classes. *(Oswald Spengler)*

A politician is a person who approaches every situation with an open mouth. *(Adlai Stevenson)*

I would walk over my grandmother if necessary to get Nixon re-elected. *(Charles Colson in 1972)*

Bill Clinton's foreign policy experience stems mainly from having had breakfast at the International House of Pancakes. *(Pat Buchanan)*

It would be desirable if every government, when it comes into power, should have its old speeches burned. *(Philip Snowden)*

If any demonstrator ever lays down in front of my car, it will be the last car he'll ever lay down in front of. *(George Wallace)*

I think Hitler was too moderate. *(J.B. Stoner)*

George Bush is a fake, a fool and a wimp. *(Jules Feiffer)*

The entire history of Margaret Thatcher is one of violence and oppression and horror. She's only one person, and she can be destroyed. I just pray there's a Sirhan Sirhan somewhere... it's the only remedy for this country at the moment. *(Morrissey in 1984)*

Winston Churchill suffered from petrified adolescence. *(Aneurin Bevin)*

Dan Quayle has two books on politics, but he hasn't finished colouring in the first one yet. *(Graffito)*

Ask not what you can do for your country, for they are liable to tell you. *(Mark Steinbeck)*

Harold Macmillan's role as a poser was itself a pose. *(Harold Wilson)*

Tony Benn - the Bertie Wooster of Marxism. *(Malcolm Bradbury)*

John Major delivers all his statements as though auditioning for the speaking clock. *(Stephen Glover)*

I never trust a man unless I've got his pecker in my pocket. *(Lyndon Johnson)*

They're not fit to manage a whelk-stall. *(Winston Churchill on The Labour Party)*

I didn't fire General MacArthur because he was a dumb son of a bitch. He was, but that's not against the law for generals. If it was, three-quarters of them would be in jail. *(Harry Truman)*

One must do the greatest good one can for one's friends, and the utmost harm to one's enemies. *(Benito Mussolini)*

Men enter local politics solely as a result of being unhappily married. *(C. Northcote Parkinson)*

The oldest, wisest politician grows not more human, but is merely a grey wharf rat at last. *(Henry Thoreau)*

Margaret Thatcher has the eyes of Caligula, but the mouth of Marilyn Monroe. *(Francois Mitterand)*

I'd go back on cigarettes, and kill Gerry Adams. *(Hugh Leonard after being asked what he would do if he was informed he had a terminal illness).*

Nixon is a purposeless man, but I have great faith in his cowardice. *(Jimmy Breslin)*

Republics show the art of running the circus from the monkey cage. *(H.L. Mencken)*

Hillary Clinton said that while the president was testifying in the Paula Jones case she was doing some household chores. Little things like sewing the president's pants to his shirts. *(Conan O'Brien)*

Scrubbing floors and emptying bedpans has as much dignity as the Presidency. *(Richard Nixon)*

A politician is a person who will double-cross a bridge before he comes to it. *(Oscar Levant)*

I do not keep a diary. Never have. To write a diary every day is like returning to one's own vomit. *(Enoch Powell)*

I have learned that one of the most important rules of politics is poise, which means looking like an owl after you've behaved like a jackass. *(Ronald Reagan)*

On behalf of the people of Ireland, I brand you a traitor and a liar. *(Ian Paisley to Margaret Thatcher in the House of Commons in 1981)*

Bernadette Devlin is Fidel Castro in a mini-skirt. *(Stratton Mills)*

If I wished to punish a province, I would have it governed by philosophers. *(Frederick the Great)*

The Treasury could not, with any marked success, run a fish and chip shop. *(Harold Wilson)*

Bureaucracy defends the status quo long- after the quo has lost its status. *(Laurence J. Peter)*

I've met serial killers and pro-fessional assassins, but nobody ever scared me as much as Margaret Thatcher. *(Ken Livingstone)*

There's one sure way of telling when politicians aren't telling the truth - their lips move. *(Felicity Kendall)*

Any American who's prepared to run for president should automatically, by definition, be disqualified from ever doing so. *(Gore Vidal)*

The trouble with Winston Churchill is that he nails his trouser to the mast and can't climb down. *(Clement Attlee)*

Greater love hath no man than this, that he lay down his friends for his life. *(Jeremy Thorpe on Harold Macmillan)*

It's not hard to find Gerry Ford on a golf course. You just follow the wounded. *(Bob Hope)*

Margaret Thatcher couldn't see an institution without hitting it with her handbag. *(Julian Critchley)*

A reactionary is a somnambulist walking backwards. *(Franklin D. Roosevelt)*

Revolution is a trivial shift in the emphasis of suffering. *(Tom Stoppard)*

Roy Hattersley is the acceptable face of opportunism. *(David Owen)*

The ideal way of opening Parliament would be to put a bomb under it and press the button. *(P.G. Wodehouse)*

Michael Heseltine should come out of the woodwork, stop waving his plastic chickens about, run his flag up the flagpole and see who salutes. *(John Banham)*

Get married again. *(Charles Haughey's advice to a woman looking for an increase in the widow's pension).*

Communism I like, but communist intellectuals are savages. *(Jean-Paul Sartre)*

I work for a government I despise, for ends I think criminal.*(John Maynard Keynes)*

Avoid all needle drugs. The only dope worth shooting is Richard Nixon. *(Abbie Hoffman in 1971)*

Nothing is so admirable in politics as a short memory. *(Kenneth Galbraith)*

Bertie Aherne changes his mind as often as his socks. *(John Bruton)*

Jimmy Carter as president is like Truman Capote marrying Dolly Parton. The job is just too big for him. *(Rich Little)*

Sometimes at the end of the day when I'm smiling and shaking people's hands, I really feel like kicking them. *(Richard Nixon)*

Too bad all the people who really know how to run the country are busy driving taxi cabs and cutting hair. *(George Burns)*

Charles Haughey is a cross between Mother Teresa and Frank Sinatra. *(Colm McClelland)*

I had a tough time learning how to act like a congressman, in fact I accidentally spent some of my own money. *(Joseph Kennedy)*

I have some good news and some bad news. The good news is that Lenin's mother is still alive. The bad news is that she's pregnant. *(Lech Walesa)*

Communism might be likened to a race in which all competitors come in first, with no prizes. *(Lord Inchcape)*

Politics is like a harlot. If you love her unsuccessfully, she bites your head off. *(Adolf Hitler)*

I couldn't have called him an s.o.b. because I didn't know he was one at the time. *(John F Kennedy on the Canadian Prime Minister John Diefenbaker)*

It's not enough for every intelligent person in the country voting for me. I need a majority. *(Adlai Stevenson)*

An Irish politician is a man who never passed the oral-anal stage of development. In other words, he's still talking through his arse. *(Hal Roach)*

Ronald Reagan used the Constitution for toilet paper. *(John Cusack)*

Ed Muskie talked like a farmer with terminal cancer trying to borrow on next year's crop. *(Hunter S. Thompson)*

Gush and Bore. *('Time' magazine on the Bush-Gore fight for the U.S. Presidency in 2000)*

Jerry Springer is singularly the most despicable person ever to run for public office in the history of Cincinnati. *(Charlie Keating)*

Springer riposted: 'OK, I'll give you maybe the top ten. But the worst ever?'

Hillary Clinton invested in sugar, hogs and cattle in 1980. She got the idea from watching her husband eat breakfast. *(Conan O'Brien)*

Castrate them with rusty nails. *(Irish politician Brendan McGahon on how he would deal with rapists.)*

I won't eat anything that has intelligent life, but I would gladly eat a network executive or a politician.
(Marty Feldman)

The main difference between politics and movies is that in politics the speeches are harder to learn. *(Ronald Reagan)*

Patriots talk of dying for their country but never of killing for it. *(Bertrand Russell)*

Filthy storyteller, despot, liar. thief, braggart buffoon usurper, monster, ignoramus, old scoundrel, perjurer, swindler, tyrant, field butcher, land pirate. *('Harpers' magazine on Abraham Lincoln)*

Nigel Lawson is to economic forecasting what Eddie the Eagle is to ski-jumping. *(Neil Kinnock)*

Kenneth Clark is to the police what Herod is to Mothercare. *(Mike Bennett)*

The most distinctive character-istic of the successful politician is selective cowardice. *(Richard Harris)*

A politician should have three hats: one for throwing in the ring, one for talking through, and one for pulling rabbits out of if elected. *(Carl Sandberg)*

Eleanor Roosevelt got even with her enemies in a way that was almost cruel. She forgave them. *(Ralph McGill)*

It was a case of dislike before first sight. *(Winston Churchill on Kitchener's relationship to him).*

In politics it is necessary to betray one's country or the electorate. I prefer to betray the electorate. *(Charles de Gaulle)*

George Washington, as a boy, was ignorant of the commonest accomplishments of youth. He could not even lie. *(Mark Twain)*

Every sentence George Bush manages to utter scatters its component parts like pond water from a verb chasing its own tail. *(Clive James)*

I don't mind Gladstone concealing an ace in his sleeve, but I object to him pretending, when exposed, that God Almighty put it there. *(George Labouchere)*

The future of a nation has often depended upon the good or bad digestion of a Prime Minister. *(Voltaire)*

The Communist Party is the biggest corporation of all. *(John Dos Passos)*

Tony Blair is a political kleptomaniac. He stole my policies. *(John Major)*

Democracy is mob rule with income taxes. *(Rodney Dangerfield)*

An empty taxi arrived at 10 Downing Street and when the door was opened, Clement Attlee got out. *(Winston Churchill)*

I wouldn't employ him as a geek in a common carnival. *(Murray Kempton on Franklin D. Roosevelt)*

President Nixon's motto was, if two wrongs don't make a right, try three. *(Norman Cousins)*

He has about as much backbone as a chocolate eclair. *(Theodore Roosevelt on William McKinley)*

A nonentity with side whiskers. *(Woodrow Wilson on Chester Alan Arthur)*

Thomas Carlyle was so poisonous it's a wonder his mind didn't infect his bloodstream. *(John Carey)*

It was like being savaged by a dead sheep. *(Denis Healey after being abused by Sir Geoffrey Howe in 1978)*

Ronald Reagan doesn't dye his hair. He's just prematurely orange. *(Gore Vidal)*

He's forever poised between a cliche and an indiscretion. *(Harold Macmillan on Anthony Eden)*

They couldn't pour piss out of a shoe if the instructions were, written on the heel. *(L.B. Johnson on the Association of American Studies)*

A socialist is a Protestant variety of communist. *(Conor Cruise O'Brien)*

Neil Kinnock's speeches go on for so long because he has nothing to say, so he has no way of knowing when he's finished saying it. *(John Major)*

When a politician changes his position it's sometimes hard to see whether he has seen the light or felt the heat. *(Robert Fuoss)*

Sergei Filatov looks as if he has two flies fucking in his mouth. *(Boris Yeltsin on his former advisor)*

The British are a gentle race - at least when you take away their guns, their queens and their kings. *(Brendan Behan)*

I would not call her an Iron Lady. I would call her a tinfoil cutty. *(Ian Paisley on Margaret Thatcher)*

You can't help feeling that if the Eamon de Valera generation had stayed home and changed the occasional nappy, Ireland might well have been better off. *(Joe O'Connor)*

If Caligula could make a consul of a horse, why should anybody be surprised if a politician makes an ass of himself? *(John B. Keane)*

They're like two drunks who can't leave a bar. *(Bill Clinton on the stalemate between Unionists and Nationalists in the aftermath of the Good Friday Agreement of 1998.)*

What did Bill Clinton say when he was asked what he wanted to do about the Abortion Bill. *'Pay it'!*

Politicians will lay down your life for their country.

What was the worst mistake Gary Hart made with Donna Rice? *He should have let Ted Kennedy drive her home.*

What's the difference between Santa Claus and Bill Clinton's political philosophy? *There really is a Santa Claus.*

Saddam Hussein is the world's only living heart donor.

Kenneth Starr to Monica Lewinsky: 'Did President Clinton ask you to lie?
Lewinsky: 'No, he asked me to kneel'.

Dan Quayle was asked what he would do if he found $100,000 on the road. 'If it belonged to a poor person I'd give it back to him,' he said.

Why does Bill Clinton like gardening? *One of his favourite hobbies is fertilising his Flowers.*

Jimmy Carter suffered from peanuts envy.

The Nixon administration was the only brothel where the madam remained a virgin.

MORE POLITICAL QUOTES

Politics is for people who are too ugly to get into showbusiness *(Bill Clinton)*

I sense that Ireland is a fully-integrated, paid-up member of a rather vulgar, interesting, fast-moving and exceedingly bracing western society which, I suggest, now stretches in a band from Tokyo through San Francisco, Los Angeles and New York. via Galway and Dublin to London and Frankfurt, and is inching its way day by day towards Moscow. *(Ivor Kenny)*

Dealing with bureaucracy is like trying to nail jelly to the wall. *(John F. Kennedy)*

The EC badly needs a laxative.
(Bob Geldof)

Home Rule is the art of minding your own business well. Unionism is the art of minding someone else's business badly.
(Tom Kettle)

The border, between the North of Ireland and the Republic is a drunken line that reels across the country and stumbles into Lough Foyle at a place aptly called Muff. In its erratic journey it swims lakes, scrambles over mountains, wades through bogs, leaps streams and rivers, and at one point rips clean through a poor man's cottage, thereby making him a subject of Queen Elizabeth when be is in the kitchen, and a son of the Republic when he is in bed.
(Brian Friel)

I never met anyone who understood the Irish question, except one Englishman who had only been there a week. *(Keith Fraser)*

The difference between Nixon and Humphrey is the same as the difference between warm shit and cold shit. *(Charles Bukowski)*

She has all the sensitivity of a sex-starved boa constrictor. *(Tony Banks on Margaret Thatcher)*

Calvin Coolidge didn't say much, and when he did he didn't say much. *(Will Rogers)*

A politician is a statesman who approaches every situation with an open mouth. *(Adlai Stevenson)*

Votes for everybody and votes for anybody is making civilisation into a rush of Gadarene swine down a steep place into the sea. *(George Bernard Shaw)*

He has a great mind - until it's made up. *(Lady Violet Bonham-Carter on Sir Stafford Cripps)*

If a tree fell in the forest and no one was there to hear it, it might sound like Dan Quayle looks. *(Tom Shales)*

A politician is a man who has nothing to say but insists on saying it anyway. *(Sean Hughes)*

The Irish who fought for that fascist cunt Franco at least had the good sense to come home with more men than they went out with. *(Brendan Behan)*

I think I can safely bet that Aristotle Onassis would not have married Mrs Khruschev if he had been assassinated like John F. Kennedy. *(Gore Vidal)*
Putting a Sinn Fein president in a government in Northern Ireland is like putting Hitler in a synagogue. *(David Trimble on Gerry Adams in 1998)*

They say de Valera is fluent in seven languages - more's the pity we can't understand him once in a while. *(Brendan Behan)*

Tony Benn immatures with age. *(Harold Wilson)*

Neil Kinnock walked backwards into socialism for the same reason the penniless man walked backwards into the cinema - in the hope that the attendant would think he was leaving it. *(Nigel Lawson)*

Edwina Currie is the Princess Michael of politics. *(Keith Waterhouse)*

As Moses, Jim Callaghan would have mis-timed his arrival at the parting of the waves. *(Austin Mitchell)*

There's a lot to be said for being nouveau riches and the Reagans mean to say it all. *(Gore Vidal)*

When they circumcised Herbert Samuel they threw away the wrong bit. *(David Lloyd George)*

Winston Churchill has devoted the best years of his life to preparing his impromptu speeches. *(F.E. Smith)*

Washington could not tell a lie. Nixon could not tell the truth. Reagan could not tell the difference. *(Mort Sahl)*

I can still remember the first time I heard Hubert Humphrey speak. He was in the second hour of a five-minute talk. *(Gerald Ford)*

An election is a moral horror, as bad as a battle except for the blood, a mudbath for every soul concerned in it. *(George Bernard Shaw)*

It was sinful that Ronald Reagan ever became president. Most of the time he was an actor reading his own lines. But let me give him his due: he would have made a hell of a king. *(Tip O'Neill)*

Every time we find an answer to The Irish Question the Irish change the question. *(Winston Churchill)*

Writing a birthday note to Lyndon Johnston is like drafting a state document. *(John F. Kennedy)*

Ireland is banjaxed and washed out. A man stood up in the audience at the 'Late Late Show' three or four years ago and said that if we had any manners we'd hand the entire island back to the Queen of England at 9 O'clock the following morning and apologise for its condition. The longer I remember that guy, the more I think he had something. *(Gay Byrne)*

Bill Clinton's definition of safe sex is when Hillary is out of town. *(Iain Dale)*

What's the difference between Dan Quayle, Jane Fonda and Bill Clinton?
Jane Fonda went to Vietnam. *(John Simmons)*

I have searched through official documents and through the files of many newspapers but in none of them could I find where Brian Faulkner had ever said a kindly word about anyone. *(Andrew Boyd)*

An Irish politician is a man of few words - but he uses them often. *(Eamon Nally)*

Dev reminds me of a cross between a corpse and a cormorant. *(Oliver St. John Gogarty)*

Henry Kissinger brought peace to Vietnam the same way Napoleon brought peace to Europe: by losing. *(Joseph Heller)*

Negotiating with him is like picking up mercury with a fork. *(David Lloyd George on the difficulty of engaging in political discourse with De Valera.)*

De Valera riposted: 'Why doesn't he use a spoon?

I believe Hugh Grant is going to visit Northern Ireland. He should find a lot to identify with here. After all, his problems began with 69 too. *(Patrick Kielty)*

Lyndon Johnson is a man of his most recent word. *(William F Buckley)*

Bella Abzug could boil the fat off a taxicab driver's neck. *(Norman Mailer)*

George Bush is a Boy Scout with a hormonal imbalance. *(Kevin Phillips)*

Spiro Agnew reminds me of the kind of guy who would make a crank call to the Russians on the hot line. *(Dick Gregory)*

Today, if Pamela Anderson wanted to run for president, I bet there'd be a few hundred thousand voters who'd think, why not. If she doesn't seem, well, awake, so what. Neither did Reagan. *(Michael Atkinson)*

Sleeping with a president used to mean you attended a Reagan cabinet meeting. *(Jay Leno)*

Clement Attlee reminds me of nothing so much as a recently dead fish, before it has had time to stiffen. *(George Orwell)*

I agree that Frank 0' Connor grows on you - like a cancer. *(Mario Procacchino, Democratic candidate for the mayorship of New York in 1965)*

Haughey would unhesitatingly roller-skate backwards into a nunnery, naked from the waist down and singing 'Kevin Barry' in Swahili if it would help him gain a vote. *(Hugh Leonard on Charles Haughey the former Irish Tauiseech)*

Stanley Baldwin takes a leap in the dark, looks around and then takes another. *(F.E. Smith)*

Coloured servants out there don't really mind. They get their food and their board, so why should they? Gosh, you get coloured servants all round the world, don't you? *(Cliff Richard giving his unique spin on apartheid after a South African tour in 1963)*

In Russia a man is called reactionary if he objects to having his property stolen and his wife and children murdered. *(Winston Churchill)*

I was thoroughly in favour of Margaret Thatcher's visit to the Falklands. I found a bit of hesitation, though, about her coming back. (*John Simon*)

Dan Quayle was born with a silver foot in his mouth. (*Jay Leno*)

I used to be in favour of women priests, but two years in the Cabinet cured me of that. *(Norman St. John-Stevas)*

Attila the Hen. *(Clement Freud on Margaret Thatcher)*

I'm going to get rid of everybody who doesn't agree with my policies. *(Lyndon Johnson in 1965)*

John F. Kennedy was more interested in gossip than in Russian missiles. *(Eddie Fisher)*

I captured some of the people who tried to assassinate me. I ate them before they ate me. *(Idi Amin)*

A politician is someone who believes you don't have to fool all the people all the time. just during elections. *(Stanley Davis)*

I'll be buggered if I join the Liberal Party. *(Nigel Rees)*

Prostitutes don't vote because they don't care who gets in. *(Roy Brown)*

Dan Quayle thinks the Gaza Strip is Paul Gascoigne's football jersey. *(Johnny Carson)*

I would never run for President. Some people have skeletons in their closets, but I have a graveyard. *(Sylvester Stallone)*

His argument was as thin as the homeopathic soup that was made by boiling the shadow of a pigeon that had been starved to death *(Abraham Lincoln on Stephen Douglas)*

Reforms are less to be dreaded than revolutions, for they cause less reaction. *(Justice Darling)*

Fleas can be taught nearly everything that a Congressman can. *(Mark Twain)*

A once-fine champion of the underdog, Ireland's Labour Party now has all the political weight of an anorexic tadpole. *(David Kenny)*

Men are brave enough to go to war, but not to have a bikini wax. *(Rita Rudner)*

No real Englishman, in his secret soul, was ever sorry for the death of a political economist. *(Walter Bagehot)*

Merely by opening his mouth he managed to snatch banality from one of the most dramatic events in the history of the world. *(Harry Browne on George Bush's reaction to the suicide bombing of New York's twin towers in September 2001).*

When Mrs Thatcher says she has a nostalgia for Victorian values I don't think she realises 90% of such nostalgia would be satisfied in the Soviet Union. *(Peter Ustinov)*

Give Charlie Haughey enough rope and he'll hang you. *(Leo Enright)*

Trying to maintain good relations with the communists is like trying to woo a crocodile. *(Winston Churchill)*

Voting Tory is like being in trouble with the Police. You'd rather the neighbours didn't know. *(Charles Kennedy)*

Not while I'm alive he ain't. *(Ernest Bevin in response to the allegation that Aneurin Bevan was his own worst enemy)*

We have always found the Irish to be a bit odd. They refuse to be English. *(Winston Churchill)*

Ted Heath is a shiver looking for a spine to run up. *(Harold Wilson)*

It was said that you could not throw a stick over a poor-house wall without hitting one of his bastards. *(Stan Gebler Davies on Daniel O'Connell)*

I could instance a load of fuck-ers whose throats I'd cut and push over the nearest cliff. *(Charles Haughey)*

It's silly talking about how many years we'll have to spend in the jungles of Vietnam when we could pave the whole country and put parking stripes on it and still be home by Christmas. *(Ronald Reagan in 1965)*

Sir Robert Peel's smile is like the silver plate of a coffin. *(Daniel O'Connell)*

I believe that Ronald Reagan can make this country what it once was...an Arctic region covered with ice. *(Steve Martin)*

If I saw Mr Haughey buried at midnight at a crossroads, with a stake driven through his heart - politically speaking - I should continue to wear a clove of garlic round my neck, just in case. *(Conor Cruise O'Brien)*

The Marxist law of the distribution of wealth is that shortages be divided equally among the peasants. *(John Guftason)*

A nasty interlude between the Bushes. *(Hitchens on Bill Clinton's presidency)*

Bill Clinton always came across as a man who knew he was. born to be president, while George Bush has the gait of one who has inherited the hand-me-down suit. *(Shane Hegarty)*

Sometimes I look at Billy and Jimmy and I say to myself, 'Lillian' you should have stayed a virgin.' *(Lillian Carter)*

I don't know what I'd do without Whitelaw. Everyone should have a Willy. *(Margaret Thatcher)*

Winston Churchill would kill his own mother just so that he could use her skin to make a drum to beat his own praises. *(Margot Asquith)*

My husband always said that his acting life was good preparation for politics. *(Nancy Reagan)*

Stafford Cripps has a brilliant mind - until he makes it up. *(Margot Asquith)*

The Conservative Establishment has always treated women as nannies, grannies and fannies. *(Teresa German)*

Ronald Reagan thought arms control was a kind of deoderant. *(Patricia Schroeder)*

If Kitchener wasn't a great man, he was, at least, a great poster. *(Margot Asquith)*

Democracy is four wolves and a lamb, voting on what to have for lunch. *(Wilma Brown)*

We women politicians have all the men out there worrying that we'll all have PMS on the same day and blow up the town. *(Barbara Carr)*

Most Conservatives believe that a creche is something that happens between two Range Rovers in Tunbridge Wells. *(Caroline Shorten)*

I always knew Lloyd George won the war, but until I read his memoirs I didn't know he'd done it single-handedly. *(Margot Asquith)*

Calvin Coolidge looked as if he'd been weaned on a pickle. *(Alice Roosevelt Longworth)*

Franklin Roosevelt was two-thirds mush and one-third Eleanor. *(Alice Roosevelt Longworth)*

Theodore Roosevelt was an old maid with testosterone poisoning. *(Patricia O'Toole)*

George Bush's problem is that the clothes have no emperor. *(Anna Quinlan)*

When Richard Nixon is alone in a room, is there anyone there? *(Gloria Steinem)*

Liberals are just as fearful as reactionaries. For every Disgusted of Tunbridge Wells, there's a Horrified of Hampstead. *(Julie Birchill)*

George Bush's email address is president@whitehouse.gov. When you email him, they send you back these wonderful messages like 'President Bush will consider your email". Will he shit. He won't even see it. But then they know where your computer is, and you're on their hit list. *(Andrea Kennedy)*

You can no more win a war than you can win an earthquake. *(Jeanette Rankin)*

War has become a luxury that only small nations can afford. *(Hannah Arendt)*

Communists are people who fancied that they had an unhappy childhood. *(Gertrude Stein)*

I don't mind how much my Ministers talk, as long as they do what I say in the end. *(Margaret Thatcher)*

Ronald Reagan promised to take senility tests, but he forgot. *(Lorna Kerr-Walker)*

My only political ambition is to be re-elected. *(Glenda Jackson)*

How could they tell? *(Dorothy Parker after hearing President Calvin Coolidge had died)*

John Major is marginally better than cystitis. *(Jo Brand)*

Gladstone speaks to me as if I were a public meeting. *(Queen Victoria)*

A woman voting for divorce is like a turkey voting for Christmas. *(Alice Glenn)*

I can't stand Republicans. They're old, stupid, bullshit-dressing pinchy-faced, golfing, bad hair day people. *(Cher)*

I've been married to a communist and a fascist, and neither of them would take out the trash. *(Zsa Zsa Gabor)*

Margaret Thatcher surprised everyone by buying a house in Dulwich instead of moving to Bolivia with the rest of the Nazis. *(Jo Brand)*

You can say what you like about Genghis Khan, but when he was around, old ladies could walk the streets of Mongolia at night. *(Jo Brand)*

Hillary Clinton is a raisin-eyed, carrot-nosed, twig-armed, straw-stuffed mannequin, trundled in on a go-kart by the mentally bereft powerbrokers of the State Deomocratic Party. *(Camille Paglia)*

Paula Jones sued President Clinton because he allegedly asked her to perform a sex act on him. In that case, every woman in America is owed millions by construction workers. *(Elaine Bosler)*

other POWERFRESH titles

POWERFRESH TONI GOFFE TITLES

1902929411	FINISHED AT 50	2.99	☐
1902929403	FARTING	2.99	☐
190292942X	LIFE AFTER BABY	2.99	☐

POWERFRESH MAD SERIES

1874125783	MAD TO BE FATHER	2.99	☐
1874125694	MAD TO BE A MOTHER	2.99	☐
1874125686	MAD ON FOOTBALL	2.99	☐
187412552X	MAD TO GET MARRIED	2.99	☐
1874125546	MAD TO HAVE A BABY	2.99	☐
1874125619	MAD TO HAVE A PONY	2.99	☐
1874125627	MAD TO HAVE A CAT	2.99	☐
1874125643	MAD TO BE 40 HIM	2.99	☐
1874125651	MAD TO BE 40 HER	2.99	☐
187412566X	MAD TO BE 50 HIM	2.99	☐

POWERFRESH FUNNYSIDE SERIES

1874125260	FUNNY SIDE OF 30	2.99	☐
1874125104	FUNNY SIDE OF 40 HIM	2.99	☐
1874125112	FUNNY SIDE OF 40 HER	2.99	☐
190292911X	FUNNY SIDE OF 50 HIM	2.99	☐
1874125139	FUNNY SIDE OF 50 HER	2.99	☐
1874125252	FUNNY SIDE OF 60	2.99	☐
1874125279	FUNNY SIDE OF SEX	2.99	☐

POWERFRESH OTHER A5

1874125171	"CRINKLED "N" WRINKLED"	2.99	☐
1874125376	A MOTHER NO FUN	2.99	☐
1874125449	WE'RE GETTING MARRIED	2.99	☐
1874125481	CAT CRAZY	2.99	☐
190292908X	EVERYTHING MEN KNOW ABOUT SEX	2.99	☐
1902929071	EVERYTHING MEN KNOW ABOUT WMN	2.99	☐
1902929004	KISSING COURSE	2.99	☐
1874125996	CONGRATULATIONS YOU'VE PASSED	2.99	☐
1902929276	TOILET VISITORS BOOK	2.99	☐
1902929160	BIG FAT SLEEPY CAT	2.99	☐

POWERFRESH SILVEY JEX TITLES

1902929055	FART ATTACK	2.99	☐
1874125961	LOVE & PASSION 4 THE ELDERLY	2.99	☐
187412597X	A BABY BOOK	2.99	☐
1874125996	SHEEP 'N' NASTY	2.99	☐
1874125988	SPORT FOR THE ELDERLY	2.99	☐
1902929144	FUN & FROLICS FOR THE ELDERLY	2.99	☐

POWERFRESH HUMOUR

1874125945	GUIDE TO SEX & SEDUCTION	3.99	☐
1874125848	DICK'S NAUGHTY BOOK	3.99	☐
190292925X	MODERN BABES LB OF SPELLS	4.99	☐
1902929268	A MUMS LB OF SPELLS	4.99	☐

POWERFRESH LITTLE SQUARE TITLES

1902929330	LS DIRTY JOKES	2.50	☐
1902929314	LS DRINKING JOKES	2.50	☐
1902929322	LS GOLF JOKES	2.50	☐
190292939X	LS IRISH JOKES	2.50	☐
1902929292	LS TURNING 18	2.50	☐
1902929977	LS TURNING 21	2.50	☐
1902929969	LS THE BIG 30	2.50	☐
1902929241	LS THE BIG 40	2.50	☐
1902929233	LS THE BIG 50	2.50	☐
1902929284	LS BIG 60	2.50	☐
1902929225	LS SINGLE V MARRIED WOMEN	2.50	☐
1902929217	LS YES BUT...!	2.5	
1902929306	LS WHISKY	2.5	
1902929500	LS HOW TO PULL BY MAGIC	2.5	

POWERFRESH STATIONARY TITLES

1902929381	WEDDING GUEST BOOK	9.9	
1902929349	WEEKLY PLANNER CATS	6.9	
1902929357	WEEKLY PLANNER DOGS	6.9	
1902929365	WEEKLY PLANNER COTTAGES	6.9	
1902929373	WEEKLY PLANNER OFFICE	6.9	
1902929519	HUMDINGER TELEPHONE BOOK	4.9	
1902929527	HUMDINGER ADDRESS BOOK	4.9	
1902929535	HUMDINGER NOTEBOOK	2.9	

Name _____

Address _____

_____

_____

P&P £1.00 Per Parcel

Please send cheques payable to Powerfresh LTD

To Powerfresh LTD 21 Rothersthorpe Crescent

Northampton NN4 8JD